Dear Reader,

Disney Editions is honored to present a facsimile reproduction ... ... treasure—the print... ...elf-published recollections of the Pirates' Code (which he considered to be more actual guide... ...) and the knowledge he acquired during his many years on the account. Author Joshamee Gibbs was First Mate to the legendary Captain Jack Sparrow, Pirate Lord of the Caribbean, and as such, he literally went to the ends of the earth and back in his adventures.

Rumors of the existence of this book have circulated for generations. Bits and pieces of Joshamee's knowledge have surfaced through the years, passed down among seafarers whose ancestors claimed to have owned or read a copy. However no complete edition of this book had ever been discovered—until now.

With the advantage of twentieth-century technology, one of the most legendary ships to be lost at sea, the *Titanic*, was located and explored, and among the many mysteries that were solved as a result of this was confirmation of the existence of Gibbs's book. Inside a highly-decorated chest was a sealed, intact copy of *The Pirates' Code*. After changing hands several times, the book found its way to an antiquarian book dealer, who happened to be the mother of an editor at Disney Publishing.

Gibbs's manual contains his interpretations of the Pirates' Code, including entries that detail proper procedure for the division of spoils and how to invoke the right of Parlay, as well as sage advice on how to live a pirate's life, encompassing such extensive topics as what to do if you are marooned on an island; the best way to walk on a ship; an encyclopedic section on ship terminology and sailing tips; and his personal stories of the many myths and legends of the sea, such as the *Flying Dutchman* and the treasure of *Isla de Muerta*.

Upon further scrutiny, the editors were even more excited to realize that this particular copy must have, at one point, been in the possession of Joshamee himself, as he made several additions before bequeathing it to an unknown recipient. It is annotated with handwritten comments on the contents, and has letters glued in between the pages from Elizabeth Swann, Will Turner, and Gibbs's captain, Jack Sparrow. Additionally, Joshamee drew artwork in the margins, folded in paintings, and, using wax and glues, placed in ephemera that related to the text.

The book you now hold is a scan of the original with minimal clean-up. We offer it for your enjoyment and education in the hope that Joshamee's words will help you to Keep to the Code!

J.R.
J.W.
New York, 2007

Dear Jackie,

As you are about to embark on your first grand adventure at sea, and my thoughts begin to turn toward Fiddler's Green, I am pleased to give you my copy of The Pirates' Code, which I hope you will find valuable in your new endeavour.

You would do well to read it from cover to cover. The knowledge and advice included will ensure rapid advancement and success. As well, over the years, I've added in some personal observations that I think will make this more enjoyable, as they have to do with a few of our common acquaintances. I've also left in some letters and sketches that always reminded me of my own grand adventures.

But I add here a most important caution. I've always enjoyed telling the stories of my time on the account, as much as I've enjoyed hearing stories from others. Once, when Jack and Will and I were in Tia Dalma's shack, seeking the location of the Flying Dutchman, she started to tell us the story of Davy Jones. The way she told it, his troubles began when he fell in love with a woman. But the way I heard it was that it was the sea he had fallen in love with, and I told her so. She countered—"Same story, different versions, and all are true."

I agree with her. The stories I'm telling are written the way I heard them or the way I saw them. You may hear the same story told a completely different way. And all you hear will be true. Even if it isnt true. (And perhaps the only person wh could understand that would be Jack Sparrow!)

May the goddess of the sea show you her favour, and though the waters may take you far away, may your heart's compass always lead you back home.

— Joshamee

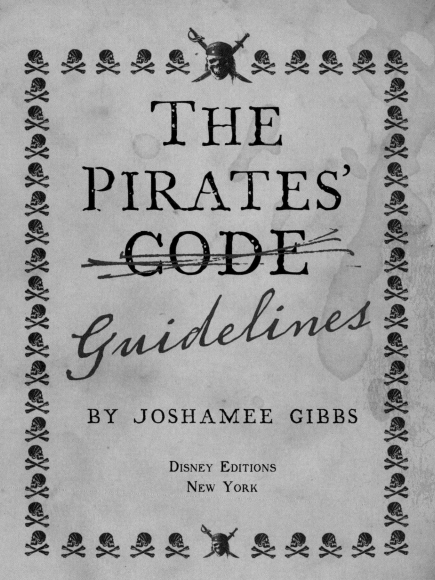

THE PIRATES' ~~CODE~~ *Guidelines*

BY JOSHAMEE GIBBS

DISNEY EDITIONS
NEW YORK

FOREWORD

As I look back on the exploits of my life, having spent most of my days at sea on all manner of vessels, honest and otherwise, I feel my hand straying towards the quill rather than the compass.

Reader, in your hands you hold one pirate's knowledge of life on the account including information academic to conducting a life at sea as well as a generalized summary of the Pirates' Code as far as I have surmised it. The Code is a sanctified instrument outlining the proper rules of engagement and protocol both on and off the high seas, among pirates as well as foes and to a lesser degree those of the friendly sort. It is my hope that this sharing of knowledge shall contribute to the community of pirates and allow each to dispense their vocation with accuracy and endurance.

THE BRETHREN COURT

Made up of the great Pirate Lords, the Brethren Court has been the governing body of the high seas as far back as the Dawn of Civilization, a time when the waters were untamed, the world a rougher place, and a sailor made his own fate.

At the First Meeting of the Brethren Court in the days before the great Hellenic society of Greece was founded, the Pirate Lords who made up this body bound Calypso, the Goddess of the Sea, in human form. They sealed her fate with Nine Pieces of Eight, so that the rule of the seas would belong to men. These Pieces of Eight are now passed down through the generations as each Pirate Lord names his or her successor to the Court.

It was at the Second Meeting of the Brethren Court that the Pirates' Code was set down by the Captains Morgan and Bartholomew and recorded in the *Pirata Codex*. The Court holds that the code is law, but through my experiences, I would consider they are more actual guidelines.

Subsequent to the creation of the Code, new members of the Court were appointed, including the Keeper of the Code who is its protector and herald. Upon request, the Keeper of the Code will interpret the Code as written, clarify points of contention, and announce his findings to the Pirate Lords. The Keeper designates his or her successor.

The Keeper is assisted by the Carriers of the Code. These two men deliver the *Pirata Codex* to the Pirate Lords when so ordered by the Keeper of the Code. This position cannot be transferred and is held until mortal demise.

At times when the very existence of pirates seems imperiled, and the Brethren wish to declare an act of war against a common adversary, they can do so only upon the agreement and the election of a Pirate King. A Pirate King is selected by a vote of the nine Pirate Lords of the Court. Prior to nomination, the King must fulfill the following three requirements: the applicant must captain a ship, swear by the code, and have killed a man. Once these prerequisites are proved, the elected King is sworn in by the Keeper of the Code. Duties of the Pirate King are detailed in the *Pirata Codex* and include declaring war, assembling forces, and fashioning strategies.

The method of summoning the Court is in the form of a song.

Hoist the Colours High

Yo, Ho haul together, hoist the colours high
Heave ho, thieves and beggars, never shall we die
Yo, Ho haul together, hoist the colours high
Heave ho, thieves and beggars, never shall we die

The King and his men stole the queen from her bed
and bound her in her bones
The seas be ours and by the powers
Where we will . . . we'll roam

Yo, Ho haul together, hoist the colours high
Heave ho, thieves and beggars, never say we die

Some men have died and some are alive
And others sail on the sea
With the keys to the cage
And the devil to pay
We lay to Fiddler's Green!

Yo, Ho haul together, hoist the colours high
Heave ho, thieves and beggars, never shall we die.

The bell has been raised from its watery grave
Do you hear its sepulchral tone?
A Call to all, pay heed to the squall
And turn your sails toward home!

Yo, Ho haul together, hoist the colours high
Heave ho, thieves and beggars, never shall we die

I've been told that the Third Meeting of the Brethren Court ended badly.

The Fourth Meeting of the Court was called by Captain Barbossa, Pirate Lord of the Caspian Sea. I was present, as were Captain Jack Sparrow and the newly instated Captain Elizabeth Swann. The East India Trading Company were advancing with an armada to destroy the world of pirates and Captain Barbossa was eager to release Calypso, a process that needed all the Nine Pieces of Eight be brought together again, in the hopes that she would bestow her favour upon him in order to gain control of the seas himself. Jack, the Pirate Lord of the Caribbean it turns out, was eager to declare an act of war against the EITC. Barbossa maintained that only a Pirate King could declare war and this was confirmed by Captain Teague—the Pirate Lord of Madagascar and Keeper of the Code.

The Keeper I saw bore an uncanny resemblance to Jack. I wonder...

There hadn't been a Pirate King as long as I could remember, since each pirate usually only votes for hisself, and they don't usually live that long, anyway (occupational hazard). But when a vote was called for, Jack changed the balance by voting for Captain Swann and as she met the requirements for the position, she was elected King. She voted for war against Lord Cutler Beckett and the EITC.

But there was so much more beneath the waterline than I could have suspected.

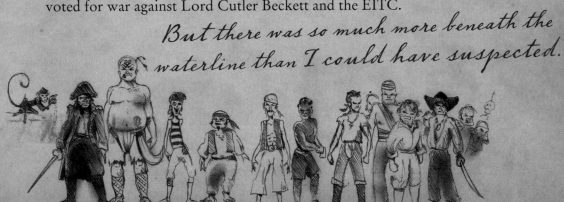

Attendees at the Fourth Meeting:

Captain Jack Sparrow

Captain Hector Barbossa

Captain Elizabeth Swann
(It's bad enough to have a woman
on board-but a captain!)

Mistress Ching
a blind Chinese woman

Gentleman Jocard
slave turned pirate

Capitaine Chevalle
says he's a "penniless" Frenchman

Villanueva
a very reserved
Spaniard

Ammand
the Corsair
scourge of the
Barbary Coast

Sri Sumbhajee
a Hindu
(with the
nastiest
bodyguards
I've ever seen)

SECTION I.

THE PIRATES' CODE

The following represents my best account of some of the topics that are contained within the *Pirata Codex*. These may not be the specific articles (because who can remember all of those bloomin' things), but I've found that in practice, these are the ones that became most important to me throughout my career.

A PIRATE'S PLEDGE

All adherents of the Code pledge to be bound together as a brotherhood of pirates, sharing alike in life's fortunes and troubles. Every member shall have an equal vote in the affairs of the moment and an equal share of the provisions. Every Pirate shall obey the Code. Anyone who fails to do so shall be marooned on a desert island, and left ashore with a loaf of bread or hardtack, a bottle of water (if any exists), and a pistol with one load.

AHOY: hello

AVAST: stop, take heed

AYE: yes

BILGE: the belly of a ship

BOOTY: treasure

BRINY DEEP: the ocean

BUCCANEER: a Caribbean pirate

BUCKO: friend

CACKLE-FRUIT: eggs

COLOURS: a ship's flag

CUTLASS: a broad, curved sword

DEADLIGHTS: eyes

FAIR WINDS: good-bye

GANGWAY: get out of my way; also a ramp on and off a ship

GRUB: food

DIVISION OF SPOILS

The Captain shall have two shares of a prize. The Quartermaster shall have one-and-three-quarter shares. The Surgeon shall have one-and-one-half shares. The Master Gunner, Carpenter, Sailmaster, and Boatswain shall receive one-and-one-quarter shares. All others shall have one share each. The Company may vote to temporarily withhold the Cook's share should his food kill a shipmate.

LUBBER: landlubber (ignorant of the sea/sailing)

MATE: friend

ME: my

SEA DOG: veteran sailor

SHANTY: sea song

SLAKE: to satisfy a craving; quench

STRIKE COLOURS: lower the flag

SWAB: to clean the deck

TACK: food; also to come about

COMPENSATION FOR INJURIES

Any pirate who has suffered an injury from pillaging, plundering, hijacking, swashbuckling, or other pirate duties shall receive compensation for the wound from the common stock.

COMPENSATION SHALL BE AS FOLLOWS, IN PIECES OF EIGHT:

Loss of right arm:	800
Loss of left arm:	750
Loss of right leg:	500
Loss of left leg:	400
Fight wound:	100
Loss of eye:	200
Loss of ear:	30 Ducats
Loss of finger:	100
Trigger finger:	200
Pinky finger:	*Life be cruel, mate*

Ragetti's eye got him 300

In the event of the loss of a limb, the Surgeon or the Carpenter may be able to restore lost appendages with what is best suited. Spare planks or other miscellaneous items found onboard may be rigged as a makeshift prosthetic. If the injury is debilitating to the point of preventing a pirate from performing his duties as an able-bodied seaman, the Quartermaster will provide a new assignment. Replacement limbs lost on duty should be compensated at no less than half-cost of natural limbs.

Ragetti
should have gotten
compensation
for having to wear
this dress...

SHARES OF PROVISIONS

Every member shall have an equal share of fresh provisions, however they may be acquired, and may take pleasure in such provisions at will, except in times of scarcity. Until said scarcity is voted over, it is necessary for the common good of the crew to adhere to rations. Anyone who takes more than his equal share of provisions at any time shall be marooned.

Any pirate susceptible of eating any foodstuff rendered pernicious shall see the ship Surgeon post haste.

Pirates should be innovative and creative, especially when it comes to cuisine. Catch-of-the-day items can include tuna, dolphin, bonito, swordfish, and mullets as well as any sea birds or doves slow enough to be caught.

The issue of fresh food is a common and regular concern for the pirate. The best way to go about obtaining fresh food is to steal it whenever and wherever necessary. When possible, acquiring livestock, such as goats or chickens, is welcome as these will provide milk and cackle-fruit for some time, and, eventually, meat. When common provisions are scarce, snakes, shellfish including periwinkles and clams, and even monkeys will provide a reasonable food source.

A Caution:

So as not to see the weevils in the biscuits!

<u>Best to eat any food that's questionably fresh in the dark.</u>

To test the freshness of an egg, see if it floats in water. If it does float, it is questionably fresh, and should be mixed with rum before eating.

Whenever and wherever possible, eat fresh fruit (limes or lemons) to avoid the scourge of <u>scurvy</u>.

You've surely got a touch of the scurvy if you're too weak for a night in Tortuga.

BASIC PROVISIONS

BEEF	CABBAGE	COCOA
PORK	APPLES	OATMEAL
RICE	FLOUR	VINEGAR
PUMPKINS	SUGAR	RUM
POTATOES	SALT	BEER
PRESERVED VEGETABLES	PEPPER	WINE
PEPPERS	SUET	AND MEDICINAL SPIRITS
ONIONS	COFFEE	WATER
PICKLES	TEA	

Additionally: iron pots, coffee mill, spices, saucepans, bowls

If you are down to your last stores, or have an inept cook, this recipe for hardtack will ensure a temporary sustenance:

Hardtack

5 parts flour

1 part water *or rum*

1 spoonful salt (if you have it)

Lard or fat

Mix ingredients and heat in a skillet until hard biscuit forms.

Lasts for months if kept dry.

Hardtack also works well as cannon ammunition.

WEAPONS

Each man shall keep his weapon, whether it be a cutlass, sword,
pistol, or other piece, clean at all times and ready for action.

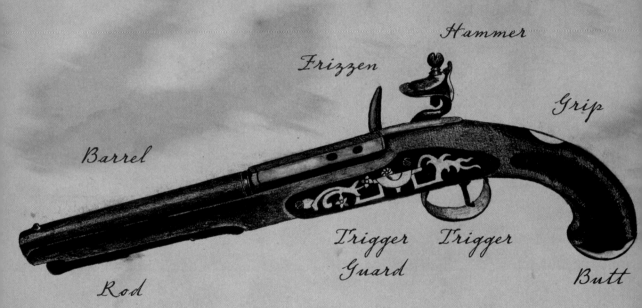

Hammer

Frizzen

Grip

Barrel

Trigger
Guard

Trigger

Rod

Butt

Jack saved the single shot in his
pistol for ten years, waiting for the
opportune moment when he would
find Barbossa in his sights

Just give your sword to Captain Turner—he'll fix it up right good for you!

SWORD

A sword is an excellent means of keeping your opponent at arm's length. Keep the cutting edge sharp and clean with a whetting stone or grinding wheel.

The cutting edge of the cutlass's curved blade also works especially well on heavy lines and canvas as well as cutting up meat, splitting coconuts, and striking a spark to start a fire.

KNIFE

The smaller size of a knife makes it ideal for carrying in one's boot, on one's belt, or in one's teeth when climbing the rigging.

Used for both cutting rope and sail, as well as for eating.

Types include the dirk, dagger, *mains gauche*, stiletto, poignard, and *boucan*.

PISTOL

Used for protection, intimidation, and as a good trading item. Also adds valuable weight when striking an opponent by hand.

Be sure to keep a small bag of gunpowder dry, or else your pistol won't do a bit of good in any battle.

AXE

Used to cut through rigging lines, open closed doors or hatches, and even assist in climbing the side of a ship. Use defensively to cut the grappling hooks of an attacking ship and in close combat.

If Will hadn't had his father's knife, he never would've cut his way out of the net filled with explosives and rum when the Kraken attacked.

Will Turner throws his axe with mighty precision.

Will Turner's Sword

SWORD FIGHTING ESSENTIALS
by WILL TURNER

He should know—made one for that traitor Norrington of folded steel and gold filigree.

LESSON ONE: CHOOSE YOUR BLADE

Selecting the right weapon for one's environment and skill level is of the utmost importance. The best way to know a weapon is to <u>forge it</u>.

A rapier or small sword would be the appropriate choice for a gentleman's duel, especially when there is ample room to maneuver. These blades tend to be long, narrow, and double-edged. However, a <u>cutlass or saber</u> is ideal for fighting at close quarters, such as onboard a ship. *Good for tavern brawls too!*

These swords have broader blades with one sharpened edge, <u>highly effective for slashing attacks</u>.

and cutting lines!

LESSON TWO: TAKE A STANCE

Learning the proper fencing stance is essential for maintaining one's balance while engaging in combat. The feet are placed shoulder's width apart and perpendicular to each other, with the leading <u>foot pointed at your target</u>. The knees are always bent, as though you are about to sit down in a chair. The shoulders and torso face away from the opponent so as to present as little target area as possible. (See Figure A)

Try that on a runaway mill wheel!

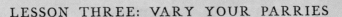

LESSON THREE: VARY YOUR PARRIES

FIGURE A

The basic fighting moves are the thrust, lunge, parry, and riposte. To thrust, one extends the sword in the direction of your target, keeping the arm straight and the palm up. This move is often followed by the lunge, which rapidly closes the distance between you and your opponent. With the leading foot, take a large step forward, bending deeply at the knee and extending with the back leg, while keeping the <u>back foot planted firmly on the ground</u>.

The parry is a defensive move, used to deflect the thrust of an opponent. <u>Variations</u> include the lateral, circular, and semi-circular parries. Always be mindful to vary parries in order to keep your opponent guessing. Follow up a successful parry with an offensive thrust, called a riposte.

Sword fighting is equal parts mental and physical. Sharpen your skills with daily practice, keep your wits about you, and <u>always try to anticipate</u> your opponent's next move.

Not if you're upside down or hanging from a boom.

Or Elizabeth's double-fisted parry!

Use any means necessary to send any scurvy bilge rat down to Davy Jones's Locker!

CLAIMING A PRIZE

If a pirate is the first to locate a prize and should find among this plunder a weapon that is better than his own, he may take it as his own. The rest of the items will be chosen in turn with the Captain first, Master second, and so forth in seniority. Ship's musicians may lay claim to any instruments found among the spoils.

RESOLUTION OF ARGUMENTS

No pirate shall strike another while onboard the ship. In the event of such an occurrence, the quarrel shall be resolved on shore by pistol, sword, or in another agreed upon manner as deemed by the Captain. Limbs or other body parts lost in duel are not to be compensated as those lost in battle.

OTHER GENERAL AFFAIRS

No man shall game for money in any form, whether it be with cards, dice, crab claws, barnacles, or any other means.

Lights and candles must be snuffed out at eight o' clock. If any man desires to drink after such time, he shall do so on the open deck without lights.

No man shall smoke tobacco in the hold without cap to his pipe or hold a candle without lantern shield. If he is discovered doing so, he shall receive such punishment as the Captain and company see fit.

And if he doesn't follow this one, fill the pipe with fish oil and let him suck on that!

While it is indisputable that a pirate's life is concerned with acquiring stores, seeking riches, and sailing and maintaining his ship, there are ofttimes when a pirate may able to pursue an entertaining diversion. Diversions may include the following:

Singing and Instrument-playing

Dancing

Reading

Shuffleboard

Crustacean ring toss

Badminton

Scrimshaw

If you cannot read, you get credit for trying, especially if it's the Holy Book, to take care of your immortal soul.

LIAR'S DICE

All players have a set of dice in a cup.

Each player turns his cup over and looks at the numbers on top of the dice without letting the other players see.

Each player in turn bluffs as to how many total units of die (ones, twos, threes) there are amongst all players.

If your bluff is called you lose.

If you bluff successfully, you win.

Some pirates have nothing to wager, save their years of servitude on the Dutchman

PIRATE
OF THE ISLES.

A hearty band I do command,
　Of Pirates bold and free,
My law is my own, my ship is my throne,
　My kingdom is on the sea ;
My flag is red, at the royal mast head,
　On all my foes I smile,
No quarter show where'er I go,
　　But the prize we soon will take in tow.
　　　　　My men are tried, my bark is my pride,
　　　　　My men are tried, my bark is my pride,
　　　　　For I'm the pirate of the Isles,
　　　　　I'm the pirate of the Isles,
　　　　　I'm the pirate, I'm the pirate,
　　　　　I'm the pirate of the Isles.

We luff a sail in a pleasant gale,
　O'er the dark and bounding sea ;
With a prize in view, we will heave her too,
　And we'll haul her under our lea ;
We'll give three cheers, then homeward steer,
　While fortune on us smiles,
None came across that famed La Ross,
　But to him they had to strike their course.
　　　　　　My men are tried, &c.

Ye Princely sons of Spanish Dons,
　With zeal and ardour burn,
Came o'er the sea, to conquer me,
　But back have never returned ;
Proud England too doth me pursue,
　At all her threats I smile,
Her men I've slain, her ships detain,
　Burnt and sunk them on the main.
　　　　　　My men are tried. &c.

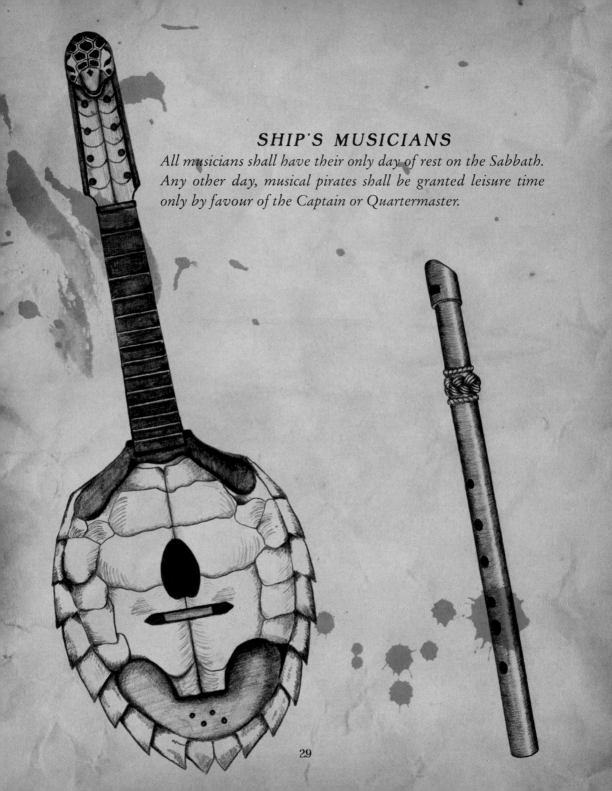

SHIP'S MUSICIANS

All musicians shall have their only day of rest on the Sabbath. Any other day, musical pirates shall be granted leisure time only by favour of the Captain or Quartermaster.

29

WARDROBE AND ORNAMENTATION

Every member of the crew shall be allowed a shift of clothes.
These may be obtained by plundering, stealing, or borrowing.

A pirate's dress includes many uses for found objects. Belts and bandoliers do more than simply hold up one's pants. They also hold ammunition, weapons, flasks, satchels, and any other small bit of plunder that can easily be strapped on and hung. Long leather coats convey ruggedness as well as serve as functional fashion as the longer tails provide extra warmth and protection against inclement weather. Shoes are optional, as they may induce slippage on the decks.

Pirate be warned—the looseness of a pirate's clothing may hide the feminine shape of a woman.

A CAPTAIN'S ATTIRE

If you are fortunate enough to be elected Captain of your ship, your position may be made recognizable by the attire you wear. The wearing of velvet, silks, gold trim, copious lace, or silver-buckled shoes will help to intimidate others, whether friend or foe, as they will most certainly be impressed by these obvious prizes you have taken.

One way to develop your Captain's apparel is to begin with your hat and work your way down. The rest of the accoutrements will follow naturally.

It is imperative that a pirate captain maintain possession of his hat at all times. When the breeze is stiff, hold on to your hat lest it blows overboard, or worse, falls into the hands of some lowly swab.*

*There are times when the wisest decision is to let the hat go.

Unless a captain must dive into the water to save a drowning wench.

Barbossa likes real big hats. Turner's got a penchant for long plumes. And Jack Sparrow... never seen a man so devoted to his hat. And how he uses it! I've seen Sparrow drink out of his, trap vicious beasts with it, and use it to protect his coins or booty.

Barbossa

Dear Mr. Gibbs,

    I was so pleased to receive your latest letter regarding the recent engagement of your sister, Margaret. Please send her my congratulations. From what you have told me of her, she must have a very sweet disposition, and I should very much like to make her acquaintance.

    As I am sure you are aware, I myself was recently bound for the altar. Unfortunately, circumstances arose that prevented the ceremony from taking place, and I found myself in possession of a wedding dress that seemingly could not serve any further purpose. Heaven forbid that any such thing should happen to your lovely sister, but on the slightest chance that she meets a similar predicament, the following counsel may prove useful.

    Should a jilted bride require transportation aboard a ship in order to rescue a fiancée in need, or merely to escape the scene of the wedding, a wedding dress can be employed as a means of influencing the ship's destination. Sailors, being quite superstitious folk, are wont to believe in the existence of ghosts, and a white wedding dress being puppeted from the rigging can instill fear in all manner of stout-hearted seafarers.

The fabric of the gown can also be utilized when patching sails or as an aid in slowing descent when jumping from ship to ship.

And in the event that a bride should find herself tragically marooned or stranded on a deserted island, a wedding dress can be fashioned into a hammock, rigged as a shield from the sun, or burned in a signal fire.

I do hope that your sister never has any cause to consult these ruminations, and please convey my wish to have tea with her at her earliest convenience.

Warm regards,

Elizabeth

Jack's Mark

HOW TO LOOK FIERCE, YET PRACTICAL

Tattoos always intimidate. Additionally, they are extremely practical, as they may record a specific time in one's life or travels, or mark one's identity lest one should be too inebriated to remember it, or be killed and rendered unrecognizable.

A rose and thorns symbolizes manly strength.

A sea creature will serve to remind you of the perils of the sea.

A snake or skull represents the underworld and death.

A sparrow means "freedom." It also indicates that a sailor has traveled a considerable amount of nautical miles.

Body art is another way to instill fear and effect an enemy's surrender. Decorating your face with extra eyes or teeth, or painting a skeletal pattern on the exterior of your skin can incite alarm and dismay.

Wear black coal, tar, or grease under your eyes. It will keep the sun from blinding you on the water, as well as darken and disguise your demeanor.

PIRATE COIFFURE

A pirate's coiffure should, above all, attempt to look menacing, whether he is adorned with locks, beard, scarf, or hat.

Beards may be utilized to hold small knives, smoking fuses, or varied devices to motivate submission. They are also useful to <u>warm the chin</u> and chest in inclement weather.

Long hair may be desired by some, but in a gale can cause dire consequences when trying to read a compass or map. Dreadlocks are easier to take care of, don't flutter too much in the wind, and are delightfully functional for stringing beads, shells, jewels, ribbons, coins, or other dangly bits such as <u>animal bones</u> or ladies' favours.

Any sundry item may be included to mark one's travels and showcase the exotic locales a pirate has visited.

Don't believe whatever Sparrow says about how he got that reindeer bone. He'd never survive the cold that long. He probably got it from Tia Dalma.

Sometimes they merely showcase lunch.

Purchased at Drake's Apothecary, Carne Lane, Tortuga

HAIR VIGOR TOILET — Restores Gray Hair to its Natural Vitality and Color.

AYER'S HAIR VIGOR

PREPARED BY DR. J. C. AYER & CO. LOWELL, MASS. U.S.A.

I thought darkening my whiskers might entice the ladies even more...

THE RIGHT OF PARLAY

If a pirate is captured by an enemy ship, he has the right to demand Parlay, or temporary protection, until he may have an audience with the enemy Captain. At this point, he cannot be harmed. Parlay is not considered concluded until said captives and Captains have completed negotiations.

It is best advised for any pirate not to get themselves into a position when Parlay would be utilized, owing to the fact that it is often an act done in desperate or difficult circumstances. However, if one does find himself in these straits, asking for Parlay might just save your skin. To master the art of Parlay, one must learn how to negotiate like a pirate—seeing to your needs above all others, unless the needs of others will benefit your own needs. It is also important to have leverage.

Once an accord has been agreed to, with either a verbal agreement or by a handshake or simultaneous nod, Parlay is complete and the arrangement must be enforced. If negotiations are not correctly adhered to, the contract is not binding.

However, failure to specify your desires, such as *whom* you are referring to, *where* you want to be put ashore, or *when* the agreed-upon circumstances will happen, may undo all your efforts. Never underestimate your opponent's ability to interpret your requests to his own advantage.

Tortuga
May 14

Dear Mr. Gibbs,

I sincerely hope that this letter finds you well and that a fair wind fills your sails. I will be most happy to elucidate on the question you posed in your latest correspondence concerning the art of persuasion and the various instances in which it may be implemented.

First, you must understand that being a woman provides its own unique sort of leverage when it comes to masterful negotiating. With a tilt of her head or a purse of her lips, a woman can turn the fiercest man into the most malleable putty. However, I also find a loaded gun to be quite helpful when I discover my quarry to be, shall we say, reluctant. For example, when I needed Lord Beckett's signature on the Letters of Marque that could ensure Will's freedom, I walked into Beckett's office equipped with my feminine wiles and a pistol at the ready.

In the event that the person with whom you are negotiating requests that you enhance your offer, I find that cocking the pistol is usually sufficient enticement.

When striking bargains with pirate captains, the same principles of persuasion apply. However, if you do not have a weapon at hand, you will find that most pirates are "disinclined to acquiesce" to your requests. Any additional leverage, such as an invaluable piece of treasure or a bit of vital knowledge, can prove indispensable in these instances.

If you are unsure of the value of your bargaining chip, merely dangle it overboard in the presence of your foe and the truth shall be revealed.

Finally, I must impress upon you the magnitude of influence and authority that is to be gained by being elected Pirate King. This is a title of the greatest consequence and brings with it the power to command a fleet of ships so vast and formidable that even the most indomitable opponent can be brought to its knees.

As you yourself witnessed, it is no small feat to take on the East India Trading Company and emerge victorious!

Nothing surpasses the leverage of a woman!

I remain your friend,

Elizabeth

ELECTION OF A CAPTAIN

The Captain of a ship is to be elected by a majority vote of its crew. If at any time a crew, with sufficient evidence, finds their Captain to be lacking in ability or offensive in nature, a new Captain may be freely elected amongst the ship's members. The Captain shall be made aware of the situation and will graciously step aside, assuming another position on the crew. Failure to follow this procedure will be deemed <u>a mutiny</u>.

The means by which he gets that ship is another story altogether!

The deepest circle of Hell is reserved for betrayers and mutineers!

A pirate Captain has the authority to hire a crew and command his own <u>ship</u>. A Captain has absolute power in battle, but at all other times he is to be governed by the desires and needs of his crew.

The Captain is to be given the use of the cabin having the greatest proportion in a ship. However, the use of this cabin is not exclusive and must be shared with crew members. Sharing of possessions extends to the Captain's mugs and plates, foodstuffs and drink, and any other belongings, with respect to sentimentality.

There are times when a Captain must go down with his ship, and there are times when a ship must go down without her Captain. I've observed that these times are to be determined by the Captain.

Does a Captain have to have a ship in order to be referred to as Captain? Jack Sparrow certainly doesn't think so. He insists upon being called 'Captain' even when his beloved Pearl is being commanded by another man.

ANY MAN WHO FALLS BEHIND
SHALL BE LEFT BEHIND

*Be warned
of spending
too much
time in the
sun—its
sure to
addle the
brain!*

In any number of circumstances, a pirate may find himself stranded on a desert island, whether it be the result of marooning, shipwreck, or some other unforeseen calamity. As such, pirates should have fundamental survival skills in order to exist for long periods of time in adverse conditions.

A pirate must tend to his food, shelter, and comfort. The first course of action, therefore, should be to build a shelter, catch fish, and tend to basic necessities to make the experience as pleasurable as possible during your stay.

Doesnt sound too bad, actually.

How to Build a Shelter

If you find yourself shipwrecked, and a substantial portion of your ship remains intact and relatively free of cannonball holes, it can be utilized as your form of shelter. If not, the following will prove useful.

1. *Find an unobstructed clearing void of rocks, tree stumps, etc. Within this area, there needs to be something to establish your shelter base—a large boulder, tree, or the side of a hill.*

2. *Collect as many dry sticks, tree limbs, or pieces of driftwood as possible. Brace the largest pieces against your base, then fill the cracks with the smaller sticks as needed. When done, the sheltered area should be wide enough to accommodate your sleeping body.*

3. *Depending upon the climate of the area, collect palm fronds, leaves, or other vegetative material, both dry and wet. Cover the shelter with the dry vegetation first, then insulate it with the wet. Muddy leaves and dirt work even better. Palm fronds may be woven to form a thatch. If you find yourself stranded in a cold region, you may use snow instead of wet leaves.*

4. *If none of the above is available, you may seek shelter in a cave or in a ditch or depression, to avoid blustery winds. However, if it rains, the latter choice may prove to be an unfortunate one.*

How to Make a Hammock

1. *Locate two tree trunks approximately one and a half times your height from each other. If no trees are available, poles may be set into the earth, possibly from broken masts or ship parts.*

2. *Procure a piece of durable fabric, preferably sail canvas. It should be large enough to contain your body.*

3. Use two pieces of line or rope or sturdy vines strong enough to sustain your weight that are each several arm-lengths long.

4. Cut several small holes along the "head" and "foot" ends of the material. Weave one piece of rope through the holes at each end. Secure each with a bowline.

5. Tie the free ends of the ropes around the trees at about chest height with a bowline or several half hitches.

6. If you have enough line, you may construct your hammock by creating a net of knots. This might also prove creative entertainment as you await rescue.

7. Climb in with a bottle of rum and let the ocean breeze rock you to sleep!

How to Open and Eat a Coconut

1. Climb a coconut tree and select a green coconut, which contains the biggest amount of coconut "water" or "milk." Be careful not to fall out of the tree, as this will delay accomplishing your task.

2. Remove the husk and take note of the three "eyes" found at the end of the coconut that resemble a monkey's face.

3. Poke through two of the eyes. One is to allow air in; the other is to allow the milk out. Pour into a container or drink directly.

4. A coconut may also be opened by using a heavy knife or implement struck against its natural fracture points, or heated in a fire until it cracks. The white, fleshy part inside is perfectly edible.

5. Toasting shredded pieces of the coconut makes a sweet supplement to any dish. Untoasted, mashed up coconut spread on the skin will soothe a sunburn.

6. Husk fibres, the "cuir," may be constructed into a rope or utilized in caulking your damaged boat. Palm leaves may be used as containers and shelter coverings. Ambitious castaways may hollow out the tree trunk to construct a small seaworthy vessel.

7. Never underestimate the entertainment value of coconuts if rescue seems hopeless. They may be fashioned into drums or the body of a musical instrument; used for and as target practice; or hollowed out to provide a home for a small animal.

How to Catch Fish

1. *Locate a place where fish are swimming. A fish will not come to your lure if there are none in the area.*

2. *Locate an attractive enticement for the fish, such as a worm, grub, bug, or shiny bauble.*

3. *Using a long pole of bamboo or wood, attach a line made of string, rope, heavy thread, etc., and at the end of that, attach a hook fashioned from a metal object, such as a pin, buckle, or wire. Attach the bait to the hook. Cover the hook entirely with the bait as to misinform the fish of your intent. Immerse the line in the water, and wait.*

4. *Once you see that a fish has taken the bait, or you feel a tug on the line, pull the line up and seize the fish. Remove the hook and put the fish in a safe place. Repeat this procedure as needed.*

5. *Fish may also be speared with a sword or knife. Guns and explosives may be a required last resort.*

How to Avoid a Monkey Attack

1. *Do not anger a monkey.*

2. *Remove any glittering, shiny, or noisy accoutrements, such as bells or jewelry. Secure long, loose hair.*

3. *Find a place to hide. While monkeys are wily, they also bore easily. They will lose interest if you do not make an easy target.*

How to Be Rescued

1. *Build a signal fire with all available flammable objects. The higher the flame, the better.*

2. *If a writing implement and paper are available, write down the best indication of your location, seal the paper in a bottle, and throw into the ocean.*

3. Make a grand escape from the island by riding on the backs of sea turtles. Weave a harness from back hair if necessary.

Not until the rum's gone!

If a pirate should have the misfortune of being marooned on an island inhabited by cannibals, he should endeavor to avoid being made the Chief.

If he is unfortunate as to be appointed Chief, he should keep in mind the following to play the part correctly until escape can be effected:

- *Makeup and wardrobe are essential*

- *Face and body paint should be lavishly applied in ways that blend in with the tropical environment*

- *Jewelry may be edible. Take advantage of this in order to feign the lifestyle. Be sure to nibble convincingly.*

- *It may help to claim to be a eunuch*

- *Look like you're enjoying living the high life*

- *Learn to speak the language*

- *When all else fails, reach for the spices*

Cannibals

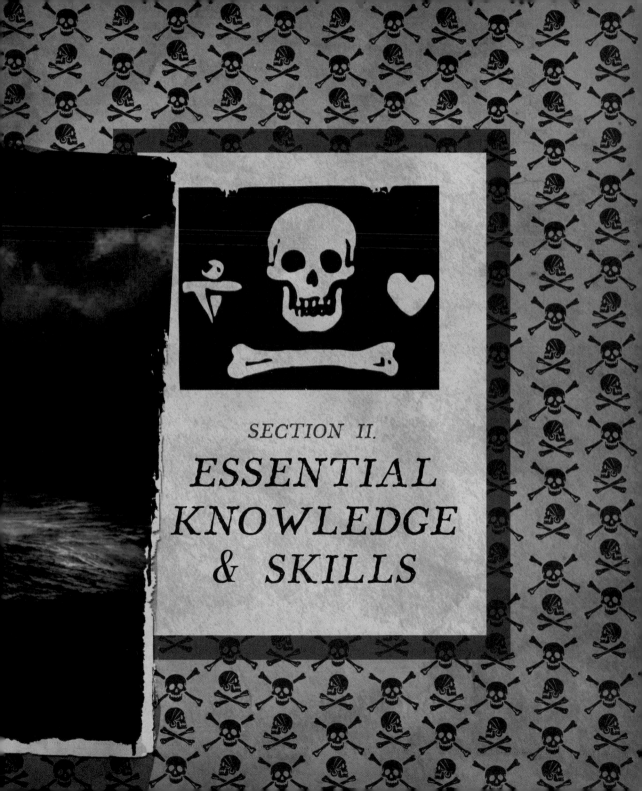

SECTION II.

ESSENTIAL KNOWLEDGE & SKILLS

Key Positions

All pirates shall serve specific duties onboard the ship, based on ability and experience. If any pirate shall lose his ability to perform his normal duties due to injuries, curses, or other ailments, then another duty will be assigned to the afflicted pirate by the Quartermaster.

Captain: Leads the crew, assumes executive authority in times of crisis, issues orders when making sail and during battle, decides which treasures to pursue and determines the best course to achieve them

Quartermaster: Liaison between Captain and crew. Settles disputes, acts as a civil magistrate and trustee for the entire crew; leads an attack against an enemy ship and/or acquires vessels; takes command of any seized provisions, treasures, or prizes and sees that they are divided fairly among the crew

First Mate: Assists the Captain in all manners, especially in the areas of navigation

Master of Arms: Maintains general order and discipline among the crew, oversees the security of the brig, escorts and guards prisoners (if any)

Gunner: Keeps ship's artillery and ammunition in order, teaches crew how to fire the cannons

Boatswain (alternate: Bosun): Keeps in his charge the ship's colours, rigging, cables, and anchors

Carpenter: Regularly examines and keeps in good repair the ship's frame, masts, yards, boats, and any other woodwork onboard

Surgeon: Procures all medicines and medical instruments, administers remedies, regularly checks on the health of the crew and attends to the wounded

Cooper: Makes and maintains all barrels and other such casks of water, liquids, and other stores

Sailmaker: Makes, repairs, and stores all sails; oversees supplies including sail cloth, twine, needles, and sailmakers' palms

Cook: Prepares food, oversees and maintains food stores

Mastery of the Ship

It is absolutely necessary that a pirate know how to sail, but not all men are well-versed in nautical knowledge before they go on the account. Proficiency in these skills will make the difference in gaining a prize or a trip to the gallows. An unskilled pirate could be a danger to the whole crew. The following is meant to familiarize an aspiring man of fortune with the skills he will need to successfully crew a ship and perhaps even one day, captain it.

KNOW YOUR WAY AROUND THE SHIP

Bow – the front of a ship, often including a BOWSPRIT—a pole extending from the bow—and sometimes a FIGUREHEAD—a decorative sculpture, oftentimes a lady or a mermaid.

Stern – the back of a ship. "The captain's quarters are typically in the stern."

I've actually seen this.

Beam – the widest part of the ship, usually about halfway between the bow and stern. "There is a <u>parasol floating</u> off our beam."

Helm – the means by which a ship is steered; either a wheel or a tiller. "The helm is on the sterncastle."

Rudder – a fin-like structure that pivots on the stern of the boat, controlled by the helm.

Hull – the body of the ship. "There were thousands of bloody barnacles on the *Dutchman*'s hull!"

Keel – a fin-like structure on the bottom of the hull that stabilizes the ship.

Sterncastle – the raised deck at the stern of a ship.

Forecastle – also fo'c's'le. The raised deck at the bow of a ship.

Though as Jack once said to me: a ship is more than just a keel and a hull and a deck. It's freedom.

DIRECTIONS

AFT – toward the stern. "The mizzenmast is aft of the mainmast."

FORE/FORWARD – toward the bow. Fore is used when referring to the sail rig—"The sails were rigged fore and aft"—or when describing an object—"The foremast is shorter than the mainmast." Forward is used in a directive sense. "The first mate walked forward to trim the jib."

ABEAM – off the beam. "The wind is currently abeam of the ship."

PORT – the left side of the ship, or to the left. "Load the port cannons."

STARBOARD – the right side of the ship, or to the right. "Turn the wheel hard 'a starboard."

ALEE/LEE/LEEWARD – away from the wind. "There are dolphins off the lee bow."

WINDWARD – toward the wind. "Look windward with your spyglass."

UPWIND – into the wind

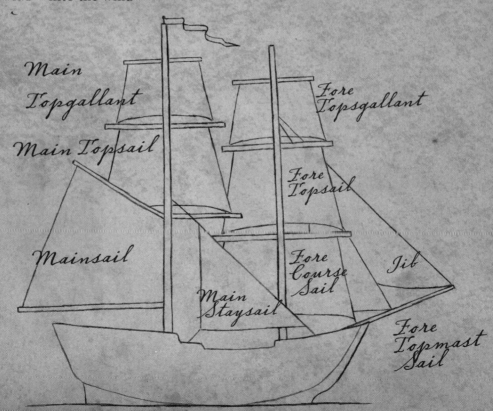

HOW TO TAKE DIRECTIONS FROM THE CAPTAIN

COMING ABOUT – turning a boat so that either its bow or stern passes through the wind. Coming about can mean either tacking or jibing. "We are coming about because the Captain's hat blew overboard."

TACKING – turning a boat so that its bow passes through the wind. "We will be tacking before we reach that reef."

JIBING – turning a boat so that its stern passes through the wind. "We're going to jibe when that island is off our beam." "Jibe-ho!"

STARBOARD/PORT TACK – the tack a boat is on is determined by which side of the boat the wind is coming from. If the wind is coming over the starboard side first, the boat is on starboard tack. "There is a ship approaching on port tack."

COMING UP – when a boat is steered closer to the wind. "Come up, helmsman" means "Point the bow closer to the wind."

FALLING OFF – when a boat is steered further away from the wind. "Fall off, helmsman" means "Point the bow further away from the wind."

If ye cant do that, then be gon with ye!

Contrary to the time I witnessed a Captain say "fall off" to a helmsman and the idgit threw himself off the boat!

POINTS OF SAIL

CLOSE-HAULED – when a boat is sailing upwind with the wind at about a 45 degree angle to the bow. "We're sailing close-hauled. If we point any higher, the sails will start to luff."

CLOSE REACH – a close reach is the next-highest point of sail. The wind comes over the bow at about a 60 to 70 degree angle. "We're on a close reach."

BEAM REACH – the point of sail where the wind is off the beam of the boat—at a 90 degree angle.

BROAD REACH – on this point of sail, the wind is coming over the port or starboard quarter, meaning that the wind direction is somewhere between a 120 and 150 degree angle to the boat.

DOWNWIND/ DEAD DOWNWIND/ RUNNING DOWNWIND – the wind is directly, 180 degrees behind the boat, or "dead astern." "We're sailing downwind." "We're sailing dead downwind." "We're running downwind."

* *Wind is always classified by the direction from which it is blowing. An East wind comes from the East, as opposed to blowing towards the East.*

IN IRONS – when a boat does not have enough speed to tack (turn the bow through the wind), she gets trapped in irons, pointing straight into the wind. To move through the water with the least resistance, a boat's natural tendency is to point bow first into the wind. "We only had two knots of speed, and when we tried to tack, the ship got caught in irons."

PARTS OF THE SHIP

RIGGING

The rigging of a ship is classified into two different categories: the standing rigging and the running rigging. The standing rigging is permanent, and the running rigging moves.

STANDING RIGGING – stays, shrouds, and other permanent parts of the rigging.

HEADSTAY/FORESTAY – a line holding up the mast that attaches to the mast at one end, and the bow at the other end.

BACKSTAY – a line holding up the mast that attaches to the mast at one end, and the stern at the other end.

SHROUDS – lines holding up the mast that attach to the mast at one end, and the sides of the ship at the other end. There are usually several for each mast, connected at various points along the height of the mast.

RATLINES – small, ladder-like rungs that are tied between the shrouds to allow a crewman to climb up the rigging.

RUNNING RIGGING – includes sheets, halyards, and other movable parts of the rigging.

SHEETS – lines that trim the sails to the angle of the wind.

HALYARDS – lines that raise and lower sails.

Pirates rarely use the word "rope" on a ship unless they're referring to the rope that dangles from the dinner bell.

Interceptor

Lines are either COILED or FLAKED on the deck of a ship, so that they can run free when needed.

When lines are secured to some part of the ship, usually a cleat or a pin, they are MADE FAST. "Bosun, make fast the main sheet!"

The anchor line (which can be chain, line, or sometimes sections of both depending on the size of the ship and the strength required) is sometimes called RODE. "How many fathoms of rode did you put out?" (A FATHOM is 6 feet.)

SPARS

SPARS include masts, booms, and yard arms.

MASTS – on a three-masted ship, the foremost mast is called the FOREMAST, the middle (and usually tallest) mast is called the MAINMAST, and the aftmost mast is called the MIZZENMAST.

BOOM – a boom is a wooden pole that attaches at one end to a mast, at a joint that permits the boom to swing around (that point of attachment is called the goose neck). Booms are used with fore-and-aft-rigged sails.

YARD – these spars are rigged perpendicular to a mast, but instead of attaching to the mast at one end like a boom, they attach to the mast at their centers. Square-rigged sails are suspended from them. They are also connected to the mast in such a way to permit them to swivel, so the sails can be trimmed according to the wind angle. The outermost ends of a yard are called yardarms.

Dauntless

PIRATES, KNOW YOUR KNOTS!

TERMS

WORKING END/STANDING END — the working end of the line is actively used to tie the knot, whereas the standing end is not.

OVERHAND LOOP — a loop of line in which the working end lies on top where the line crosses itself.

overhand knot, figure-eight knot

BIGHT — an open loop in which the line does not cross itself.

BEND — used to <u>tie two lines together</u>. *reef knot, sheet bend*

STOPPER KNOT — used to prevent a line from pulling through an opening.

LOOP KNOT — used to form a loop, whether it be fixed or adjustable.

bowline, butterfly knot

FIGURE-EIGHT KNOT — a stopper knot ideal for preventing a line from running through a block or pulley.

STEP A. Make an overhand loop with the working end of a line.

STEP B. Pass the working end around the back of the standing end.

STEP C. Pass the working end through the original overhand loop and pull tight.

When searching through another's sea chest, look closely at the knot it's secured with. If the ends be coming out on different sides, it be a thief knot. Be sure not to tie a reef knot in its place after the booty's been pilfered!

REEF KNOT – used to tie together two lines of similar thickness and material.

STEP A. Cross the working ends of two lines, keeping the right-hand line on top.

STEP B. Pass the working end of the right-hand line underneath the standing end of the left-hand line. The original right-hand line will now be in the left hand, and vice versa.

STEP C. Cross the working ends of the two lines, keeping the new left-hand line on top.

STEP D. Pass the working end of the left-hand line underneath the right-hand line. Pull tight.

*Note that both working ends should be on the same side of the knot.

Same as a square knot!

SHEET BEND – used to tie together two lines that are of different thickness or material.

STEP A. Take a bight of the thicker line in one hand.

STEP B. Pass the thinner line up through the underside of the bight.

STEP C. Cross the thinner line over the far side of the bight, and then pass it completely underneath the bight.

STEP D. Pass the thinner line under itself where it crosses the top of the bight.

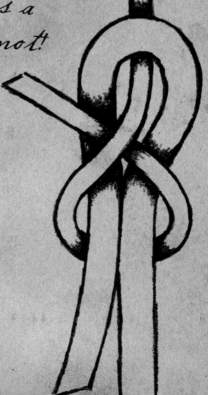

BOWLINE – creates a non-adjustable loop, and best for attaching lines to the <u>cringles</u> of sails. *That's eyes or grommets.*

STEP A. Make an overhand loop with the working end of the line.

STEP B. Pass the working end through the cringle and back through the underside of the original overhand loop.

STEP C. Pass the working end around the back of the standing end, and then through the top side of the original overhand loop. Pull tight.

MONKEY'S FIST – used to weight the end of a line so it can be thrown more easily. It can be made larger and heavier by placing an object such as a stone or marble inside.

Makes for a fine impromptu weapon in the event of attack or raid.

STEP A. With the working end of a line, make three concentric loops.

STEP B. Wrap the line three times around the middle of the three loops created in Step A.

STEP C. Pass the line through the first set of loops, and then wrap it three times around the second set of loops, passing through the first set of loops with each wrap.

STEP D. Work the strands until they are tight, or insert a circular object and then tighten.

THE SHIP'S COLOURS

The Boatswain shall be responsible for maintaining and hoisting the ship's colours; however, each member of the crew shall at every opportunity take advantage to acquire more flags for the ship. All flags retained from enemy vessels or other countries shall be turned over to the Boatswain for storage.

If "Hoist the Colours!" be called, the ship's flag shall be raised. The Captain may also call "Hoist False Colours!" whereupon the flag of a particular nation is raised in order to give any nearby vessel of that specific nation the impression that your ship is from the same country. This encourages a friendly trust and an opportunity for your ship to get closer before true colors are revealed. Or the Captain may wish to send a more intimidating message to an enemy ship by flying the red flag, the "Jolie Rouge," the colour of which symbolizes the blood of previous conquests. Circumstances will often dictate the best "ruse de guerre."

While flying a friendly flag is a useful plot, other strategies to entice potential quarry would be to dress as alluring females or act as reckless drunkards, although the latter may not be a calculated ruse if the crew is bored or uncontrollable. Methods to induce fear include throwing stinkpots, bilge water, or hardtack biscuits.

If the attack is successful, encourage the surviving crew of the captured ship to join your ranks. If they say no to this opportunity, send them to the bottom of the sea.

Meanings of the symbols used on flags I've seen

DAGGER = battle

HEART = life

BLEEDING HEART = death

ARM WITH SWORD = power

HOURGLASS = Your time is up!

PLAIN RED FLAG = no mercy

SKULL AND CROSSED BONES = death

SKELETON = death

DANCING SKELETONS = dancing with death

CROSSED SWORDS = death

DRINKING GLASS = a toast to death

ANY COMBINATION OF THE ABOVE = any resistance will result in capture or death!

Especially for a pirate who doesnt want to lose his cargo of booty to the swirling depths!

NAVIGATION

Whether he uses a compass or the stars, a pirate must always be able to find his way at sea.

NAVIGATIONAL TOOLS AND TERMS

COMPASS— an instrument used to find direction at sea or on land. Some compasses are comprised of a magnetic needle that rotates above a circular disc marked in degrees and directions, 0° being North, 90° being East, and so forth. Since the needle will always point North, a navigator can figure his course from the position of the needle. Other compasses are made with a disc that sits on a bed of fluid. The disc is embedded with a magnet so that it will rotate to indicate the navigator's orientation.

CHART— a map of the ocean and coastline, usually including a compass rose and a distance scale. Charts often identify reefs, currents, and water depths.

PARALLEL RULES— two rulers joined at both ends by metal brackets so that they can slide freely across a chart and always remain parallel. This instrument is used to trace course lines and bearings.

DIVIDERS— a scissor-like apparatus that can be adjusted to measure a certain distance on a chart.

LOG— device comprised of a piece of wood with a long rope attached. The rope has knots tied in it at a measured interval so that when the log is thrown over the stern, the number of knots passing by in a given amount of time can be used to determine the ship's speed.

KNOT— unit of measurement meaning one nautical mile per hour, used to indicate a ship's speed.

ASTROLABE— a circular instrument with a sighting arm, typically made of brass, used to calculate a ship's latitude by measuring the altitude of the sun or a star. Should be used in conjunction with celestial tables.

SPY GLASSES— used to magnify objects at a distance.

Size matters!

There be one compass that doesnt point North—Jack Sparrow's. It points to your hearts one true desire, but your heart must be sure what that is before the compass can point to it.

PLOTTING POSITION

<u>FIX</u> – a ship's position on a chart determined with the use of a compass or celestial navigation. It is marked with a circle.

USING A COMPASS

TAKING BEARINGS – with a handheld compass, determine the bearing to a charted, permanent landmark (like a fort or the coast of an island). Two different bearings are required to plot a fix.

PLOTTING A FIX – situate the parallel rules on the compass rose, aligning them with the bearing of the first landmark. Slide the rules over to the charted landmark and trace along the edge of the rules with a pencil. Repeat with the second landmark. The intersection of the two lines is the position of the ship. Circle it.

CELESTIAL NAVIGATION *The North Star is best!*

TAKING A SIGHT – when the sun or a <u>known star</u> is clearly visible, use an astrolabe to determine the altitude of the heavenly body. This is done by rotating the sighting arm, or alidade, of the astrolabe so that it measures the angle between the horizon and the chosen star.

Much easier to plot after ye've had a spot of rum

Calculating latitude – consult a current almanac of celestial tables in order to find the declination, or position in relation to the equator, of the chosen star for the date on which the sight is taken. Use this formula to calculate the ship's latitude: Declination – 90 + Altitude

DEAD RECKONING

When it is cloudy and there are no permanent landmarks in sight, this method of navigation can be used to estimate a ship's position. Position the parallel rules on the compass rose, aligned with the course the helmsman has been steering since the last plot was done. Slide the rules over to the last plotted position, and trace along the edge of the rules with a pencil. Taking into account the average speed of the ship as determined with a log, calculate the distance traveled since the last plot was done. Open the dividers so that they measure the corresponding distance on the chart's distance scale. Place one of the dividers' tips on the last plot mark. The place on the course line where the other tip falls is the ship's position. Mark it with a semicircle

Sometimes you have to set sail without knowing your heading. I've seen Jack Sparrow do that once, but it was not like him. Not at all.

WEATHER

Pirates should be prepared to face adverse weather conditions from nary a breeze to a full-force typhoon. The nimble, strong, and quick-minded pirate is the one who shall prevail. It takes a seasoned sailor to make way when there is no wind in the sails, and an ironclad-stomached one to keep the ship afloat when navigating rough seas.

MAXIMS TO HEED:

Red sky at night – sailors' delight.
Red sky at morn – sailors take warn.

A ring round the moon shall bring rain or snow soon.

If the salt is sticky and gains weight,
'tis sure to rain before too late.

Fish bite least when a wind comes from the East.

Expect a storm when ropes are hard to untwist
or candlewicks smolder.

When seagulls move inland quickly,
batten down the hatches.

Mackerel skies and mare's tails make lofty ships carry low sails. That means more rain

I told Jack that we should drop canvas when we were pursuing the Black Pearl through a tempest to Isla de Muerta. But the progress of the Interceptor had put him in a fine mood, and he refused to lose the ground we had gained.

FOUL WEATHER!

SAILING ON ROUGH SEAS

A wise Captain should know when to use a gale to his best advantage, and when to heave to and ride out a storm. It is always best to take large waves at a 45 degree angle from the bow in order to prevent the ship from being swamped. If a ship is broadside to large breakers, she may founder. In order to prevent losing control of the ship or tearing sails, reduce sail area in high velocity winds. If necessary, furl all sails.

When a <u>hurricane</u> is brewing, it is best to find the nearest port as quickly as possible. If you find your ship caught in a maelstrom, it is best to sail towards the outer edges of the whirlpool. The further towards the center you go, the more difficult it will be to escape.

Norrington clearly did not heed this advice when he was in pursuit of the Pearl off Tripoli.

Caring for Your Vessel

SHIP MAINTENANCE

In order to be protected from the elements, a ship requires constant maintenance. <u>Any sailor worth his salt</u> should be well acquainted with the practices of varnishing, tarring, caulking, and sailmaking.

Unless he be agreeable to procuring a new ship when his vessel sinks beneath him!

CAREENING – Beach the ship on shore every few months and scrub down the hull to remove any <u>barnacles</u> and other accumulating sea growths. These attachments only serve to slow down the vessel and compromise timeliness to acquiring pirate booty.

This might be a tad difficult if the entire crew is barnacled to begin with!

VARNISH – is a sealant applied to wood that makes it resistant to absorbing water. This is important because <u>when wood becomes saturated with water, it begins to rot and lose its strength.</u>

Apparently not in use on the Flying Dutchman.

CAULK and TAR – are inserted between the planks of a ship's hull in order to prevent water from seeping through the cracks. The caulk is cotton cord, chiseled into the cracks and then saturated with tar to make it watertight.

SAILMAKING – In addition to needles and thread, a sailmaker's palm is an indispensable tool in constructing and repairing sails. This leather apparatus slips over the thumb and fits around the hand, serving as a sort of thimble used to push needles through thick canvas.

SECTION III.

LIFE
AT SEA

PERAMBULATION

I'd've preferred to title this "So that's why Jack Sparrow walks that way."

A pirate must know how to walk on ship, to avoid being tossed at the crest and trough of every wave.

TO DO SO:

Walk like a duck. *(but mind waddling!)*

Turn toes slightly outward.

Keep knees slightly bent. *which may change depending*

Maintain a wide stance. *on the size of the waves*

Allow a level of buoyancy with each step.

Seasoned pirates have come to rely on the roll of the sea in order to be sure of their steps. However, this makes it difficult to regain proper composure when it comes time to use sea legs on land.

TO DO SO:

Take said sea legs straightaway to a local tavern.

Apply rum.

Notice I didn't say whether ye are rubbing it or drinking it?

Legs should work properly.

If not, apply more rum until they do.

POSSIBLE
TRANSLATIONS OF

Cotton's parrot:

If he says "Wind in Your
Sails" it means "Aye."

If he says "Anchors Aweigh" he means "I'm in."

"Any port in a storm" — he's
content with the outcome.

"Abandon
ship!" — he's
being critical.

If he says "Walk
the Plank," be sure
it's not directed
at the Captain.

"Shiver me timbers"
= you have neglected
something.

If he says "Mind the Boat," he means "Don't eat me."

If he says "Don't eat me," he really means it.

I can't figure how Cotton trained the parrot to speak
for him after he lost his tongue, but rumblings have
been made to the effect that Cotton and his parrot
might have actually switched minds!

CARING FOR YOURSELF: ILLNESS

A pirate should never underestimate his capacity for illness. There are many common ailments that can afflict a pirate while at sea. Sailors should be mindful to watch for symptoms and see the Ship Surgeon for medical care if treatment is needed.

If anyone aboard ship shall be unable to perform his duties due to ailment, see the Quartermaster for a new assignment.

MAL DE MER OR SEA SICKNESS
SYMPTOMS:
- Green under the gills
- Unable to keep food or water down
- Drowsiness
- Fatigue

REMEDIES:
- Send afflicted on deck to look at the horizon
- Salty crackers or hardtack
- Green apples (if available)

SCURVY
SYMPTOMS:
- Bruises, especially on the legs
- Inflammation of the gums
- Pain in the joints
- Thinning hair

REMEDIES:
Limes, oranges, lemons, and other citrus fruits should be incorporated into the diet.

If you are going to be sick, it is best to do so on the leeward side of the ship so that any unpleasantness will be carried away by the wind.

Best bath I ever had was in Singapore—to have a personal hot tub the way some pirate lords do.

CARING FOR YOURSELF: HYGIENE

Pirates should attempt to look after matters of hygiene, lest they become too offensive to their fellow seamen. Inattention to matters of personal cleanliness may result in various ailments and disease.

According to the ship Surgeon, most diseases are entirely in our power to prevent. Common afflictions can be warded off by adhering to the following:

If a mate falls out of shape, send him up to the crow's nest every day to gather eggs!

EXERCISE. This is very important for keeping the blood pumping and the humours balanced.

One advantage to walking the plank!

FREQUENT BATHING is necessary in preserving one's health, and should be exercised whenever in a port of call. Fresh water is preferred; however, sea water is an <u>acceptable solution</u> when it is the only option.

ATTENTION TO CLOTHING: <u>Exposure to filth and decomposition</u> has not infrequently contributed to contamination and disease.

All the more reason to be mindful of scavenging articles of clothing off the dead!

ORAL HYGIENE: Rotting teeth and malodorous breath may be symptoms of ill health. Attention to teeth and gums will improve one's overall well being. Green apples are particularly effective for pirates afflicted with offensive exhalation, especially those with gold teeth.

And if you can't find an apple, rinse with rum!

A PIRATE'S CONDUCT

A pirate should, by all accounts, do the right thing for his personal well being. Determining what is right, of course, varies upon the situation at hand. For example, one may fight fair, or one may chose not to fight fair if, in fact, one is doing the wrong thing for the right reasons. Keep in mind that in a fair fight, a pirate might be easily killed. Surely, that is not right. Therefore, there is no incentive to fight fair.

A fair trial for a mate, who by all accounts has done nothing wrong, save rescuing a damsel in distress, might indeed end up in a trip to the gallows in Port Royal. The meaning of fair clearly depends upon whom you ask.

As Jack once said, "One good deed is not enough to redeem a man for a lifetime of wickedness, but it seems enough to condemn him."

Dear Mr. Gibbs,

As we go our separate ways in Singapore to carry out the various aspects of our plan, I think back to our recent conversation about the concept of a man's moral compass and how it has caused me to ponder my own ethical bearings.

If I had been asked a few years past whether I considered myself a righteous man, I would have unwaveringly answered 'yes.' I would give the same answer today, but I do not believe that my former self would have the same perception of my present self. Thusly, it must stand to reason that the orientation of my moral compass has changed substantially.

I can pinpoint the precise day upon which this change began to take place. And it is no coincidence that it was the day that I chose to form an allegiance with Captain Jack Sparrow. I confess that my actions were driven solely by my determination to rescue Miss Swann. But that determination transformed me into the very thing I had believed myself to despise: a pirate.

It is hard to believe that I once found it near impossible to accept that my father could be both a pirate and a good man, for I have now become an embodiment of the very same paradox. Initially I worried that this fact would lessen Governor Swann's estimation of me, but I am heartened to know that we seem to be in accord.

When I saved Jack from the gallows and it appeared that I might be destined for a similar fate, Governor Swann spoke these words of wisdom: "Perhaps on the rare occasion pursuing the right course demands an act of piracy, piracy itself can be the right course."

For me at the present, the right course means saving my father from his servitude aboard the Flying Dutchman. I fear that it is creating distance between me and Elizabeth, but I hope she understands that I still love her and must do what my conscience dictates.

Your very good friend,

William Turner

THE FAITHFUL BRIDE
A Tavern of DISTINCTION
SHOAT ALLEY, TORTUGA

Di-stink-tion!

Joshamee,

After you so unceremoniously pitched off the bench last night following my seventeenth toast to the successful taking of our latest prize, then rolled into a comfortable position under the table (providing a lovely footrest!) and proceeded to snore louder than the flapping of an undertrimmed jib in an irritable wind, I spent some time musing on the subject which I had noticed to be the theme of our discourse throughout the evening—that of honesty. As I sit here finishing off your rum, I will commend my reflections to paper.

Thought the first: It's best to tell the truth, especially when you know the one you're telling the truth to wouldn't believe the truth even if you told it to him. I tell the truth quite a lot, yet people are always surprised.

Thought the second: A dishonest man you can always trust to be dishonest. Honestly, it's the honest ones you want to watch out for—because you can never predict when they're going to do something incredibly stupid.

Thirdly—Illusions of honesty are often as necessary as the actuality of honesty. Many years ago, when I proclaimed my intention for the inhabitants of that delightful town in Nassau to hand over their valuable commodities immediately or ruin and death would ensue, little were the trusting residents aware that I had not a single shot in my gun nor any other essential weaponry that should have warranted their concern. I merely appeared completely sincere and was rewarded generously for the effort.

Forthly, in my dealings, if there be two men, and, among the two men, one of them is known for committing a deviousness against the other, then it is the word of the man who has not committed that deviousness that you'll be trusting. Meaning that if it comes down to Barbossa and any other man, take the word of any other man.

However, as important as honesty can be to being able to live with oneself, having written all this, I have encountered one additional lesson in my travels regarding possessing an honest streak that would teach anyone to avoid that veracious aspect at all costs. My honesty and trustworthiness led me to the loss of my dear ship on far too many occasions—first to Cutler Beckett when a deal regarding the contents of a cargo I was to deliver proved fraudulent on his behalf; secondly to Barbossa when he tricked me out of revealing the coordinates for Isla de Muerta and the treasure of Cortés, marooning me on a barren spit of land; and thirdly to Davy Jones's terrible beastie. This last occurrence of me evidencing this cumbersome virtue of honesty also led to my death, which I honestly wish could have been avoided. A worse deal for Barbossa I think! Although three days of nothing but rum might have killed Jack then and there!

As I take leave of the virtues of Tortuga, I hope this note finds you at the farthermost position from jail and on your way to enjoying the rest of your spoils, although I'll readily admit to borrowing some remittance from you for the use of a room and a good wench as your girth beneath the table impeded my ability to share said undertable position for my own repose. The borrowing of this coin without permission should not be construed as stealing, as in my heart I have every intention of <u>paying you back</u>. I might tell you of my destination and its purpose, for I know you would now believe me whatsoever the description, but let me just offer that it includes a cask of sea sponges, an elephant, and several bottles of glue.

Your sincerest friend,

Captain Jack Sparrow

More'n likely Jack said that to AnaMaria about the Jolly Mon! Well, that's money I'll not be expecting to see again.

LUCK AND SUPERSTITION

Proper respect must be shown at all times for your vessel and the powers that be on the high seas. Mind your comings and goings, or else you'll be welcoming a host of trouble.

1. Whenever you step aboard a ship, be sure it's on the starboard side, no matter the inconvenience. Once onboard, spin around to leeward, as to make certain you're not bringing any trace of bad wind aboard.

2. Never whistle onboard. It's a surefire way of attracting unwanted wind and spirits.

3. If a ship's bell should ring without human aid, 'tis an omen of death.

4. An overturned bowl anticipates an overturned boat.

5. A school of porpoises swimming around a ship brings good luck.

6. Golden earrings bring better eyesight.

7. A piece of silver under the masthead and a piece of gold under the keel will ensure a safe voyage.

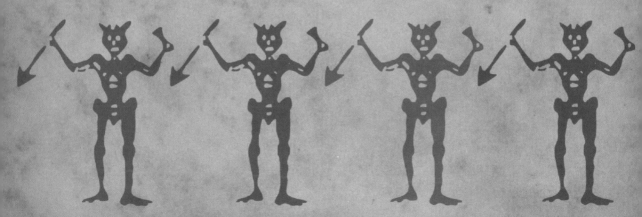

8. <u>Finding</u> and tossing a coin into the winds before sailing brings favorable weather.

"Finding" someone else's coin may bring unfavorable fisticuffs.

9. It is unlucky to change the name of a ship after its first berthing.

10. Most every pirate knows a <u>woman</u> onboard a ship brings nothing but bad luck.

Even a miniature one

THE BLACK SPOT

If the Black Spot should appear on your hand or elsewhere upon the body, it is a sign that you have been marked for death.

IF YOU SHOULD FIND YOURSELF AFFLICTED WITH THE BLACK SPOT:

Remain calm.

Wrap the afflicted area to avoid it being seen. (In some cases you may receive the Black Spot written on a piece of paper. Destroy it.)

Try not to bring unwarranted attention to yourself.

In the event that you observe the Black Spot on a fellow mate, brush the evil from your chest, turn three times widdershins (to port), then spit on the ground.

If something vexes Jack Sparrow, it bodes ill for us all.

Jack once told me a tale from his youth when the crew of the Barnacle, his first ship, came under the spell of a siren song. Jack made a deal with the sirens to release his shipmates by promising to give them his greatest treasure. Well, only a young Jack Sparrow would have made a deal like that! He should have stuffed wads of cotton in his ears! I wonder if he ever made good on his promise.

BESTIARY

MERMAIDS

These lovely creatures dwell in the depths of the ocean and look like women from the waist up, but below the waterline they have long tails covered in scales. Some have described mermaids as vain beings who spend much of their time singing and combing their long, beautiful hair. Others tell of mermaids who save sailors from drowning.

SIRENS

Sirens also appear to be beautiful women, yet they possess voices so unearthly that men can be driven to madness or even death by listening to their haunting song. These creatures perch on rocky islands, oftentimes in groups of three, singing their ethereal harmonies and luring sailors into treacherous waters. Many men have been so captivated by the sirens' song that they have run their ships aground and perished in watery graves.

ck assured
me that the
Kraken's
breath wasnt
quite that
bad.

KRAKEN

A Kraken is an enormous beast of Nordic origin that resembles a squid of gigantic proportions. Its sheer size gives it the ability to drag even the greatest of ships down to crushing darkness and its <u>breath</u> is said to smell like the rot of a thousand corpses. Its giant tentacles will suction a man's face clean off. One Kraken was controlled by Davy Jones, who bid the colossal monster to locate those who didn't pay their debt to him.

SELKIES

Selkies are seals that can shed their skins and transform into humans. In order to turn back into seals, they need only to don their seal skins again. Take care not to fall in love with a selkie. They are reputed to be quite beautiful in their human form, but they shall always long for the sea and will transform back into seals whenever they feel the call of the tide.

I heard
told the
story of a
man who
fell in love
with a
selkie and
stole her
seal skin
to keep her
in human
form.

SECTION IV.

~~BEYOND~~

~~THE SEA~~

Here Be Monsters!

A PIRATE MIGHT EXPLORE to the edges of the map and record all that he has seen, but as exhaustive a search as that may be, he will nary touch bottom for all the sea shrouds in concealment. As boundless as the sky, as luminous as the heavens, as deep as hope, as fierce as a murderous squall—the sea is all this and more. Civilizations will rise and fall but the sea will continue, as fathomless as time. It will nourish and it will destroy. In addition to the perils of reef and rock, storms and tides, there are dangers and rewards that offer no interpretation but that there is more than our pitiful mortal soul could ever understand. This magick, born of the primal waters and flowing through every waterway, is both foul and fair. Be warned and be respectful.

Much like a woman!

Thus, the sea is an <u>enigma</u>. It can humble the most daring of sailors with its wrath and unpredictability. And yet a sailor will always endeavour to tame it. An intelligent pirate knows that the sea must be respected, for there are all manner of mysteries that lie beneath its surface.

This section recounts some of the adventures I've had, individuals and entities I've encountered, and curiosities I've seen in my travels across the boundless blue. These are merely one man's stories, and by no means doctrine, but I hope that they serve to entertain and shine a light on the darker corners of the chart.

SUPERNATURAL ITEMS

Throughout your travels you will encounter objects that cannot be explained by traditional means. These objects may have special powers. Often, they may look like nothing remarkable, but their abilities should not be underestimated. A basic rule to be observed is that *belief* in the object is as important as the function of the object itself. It would be wise to keep a record of what you have seen and the talismans you may have found or taken. Here are some that I have placed down for your interest:

I dont know if there really was anything special about the dirt or the jar, but I've learned that the value of an object isnt always apparent at first glance. But believing that the object will help you can give you the courage to explore uncharted waters. With the places I've been to since I signed up with Jack, I'll take anything that might help!

I've heard that some magical objects change according to your need. Captain Jack Sparrow once told me about a set of keys that would open any lock you wanted it to. *Of course, you have to be able to get a hold of the keys before you can use them.* Jack Sparrow has a compass that points to what its bearer's heart desires. But in using it, he or she may be surprised to find out what it is that they truly want. You may be sure you want one thing, and it will show you another.

Tia Dalma gave Jack Sparrow a <u>Jar of Dirt</u> in order to protect him from Davy Jones, explaining that "land" is where Jack would be safe and so he should carry "land" with him. Initially, Jack seemed dismayed. She taunted him that if he didn't want it, then he should give it back. But her threat seemed to convince Jack that the Jar of Dirt was more than dirt.

DIVINATION

There may be times when it is essential or unavoidable to learn about one's future endeavours. There are many commonly known objects that are useful for the art of insight into the future, which would include mirrors, bowls of water, crystal balls, cards, or tea leaves. The procedure is to stare at the object until an answer is received.

I've done a lot of staring into tankards and the only future I saw was another round!

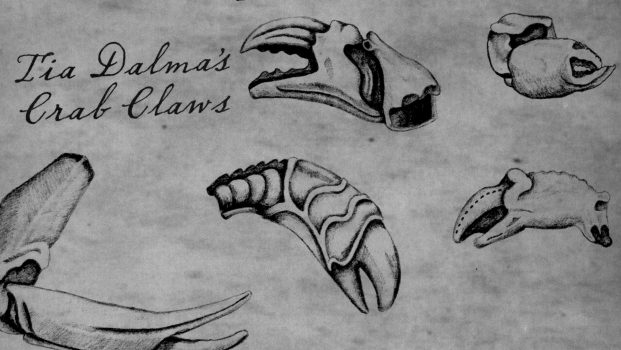

Tia Dalma's Crab Claws

THE REALM OF THE DEAD

FIDDLER'S GREEN

If a pirate has made his apologies for his wayward life, and sought and received pardon for his misdeeds, he may be fortunate enough to be offered residence in Fiddler's Green at his Final Judgment. Here there is eternal calm and joy. Here, the fiddler's fingers never rest and dancers never tire.

To get to Fiddler's Green, an old pirate puts his oar over his shoulder and walks inland until he reaches a place where the villagers ask him what he is carrying. There he will receive a bottomless mug of grog, an eternally smoking pipe, and a seat in the sun at the local inn where he can watch beautiful maidens dancing for the rest of time.

DAVY JONES'S LOCKER

An unseasoned salt may be wont to believe that Davy Jones's Locker is merely the bottom of the ocean—the final resting place for sailors lost at sea. But I can attest that the true meaning of the Locker is as difficult to pin down as a loose sheet in a hurricane.

Davy Jones will send a dying tar to the Locker if he refuses Jones's offer of servitude aboard the *Flying Dutchman* to delay his Final Judgment or if he crosses the evil captain. Since condemnation to this location is based on Jones's punishment of the sailor in question, I assume that the nature of the Locker is a manifestation of each man's personal Hell. For Jack Sparrow, it was a vast desert where the *Pearl* sat, unable to sail.

After rescuing Jack from Davy Jones's Locker, we came upon the Kraken, lying dead on the Black Sand Beach. I wonder how it got there. . . .

"Over the edge, back over again, sunrise sets at the flash of green."

Barbossa says it's not getting to the land of the dead that's the problem— it's getting back!

He also said that you have to be lost to find a place that can't be found!

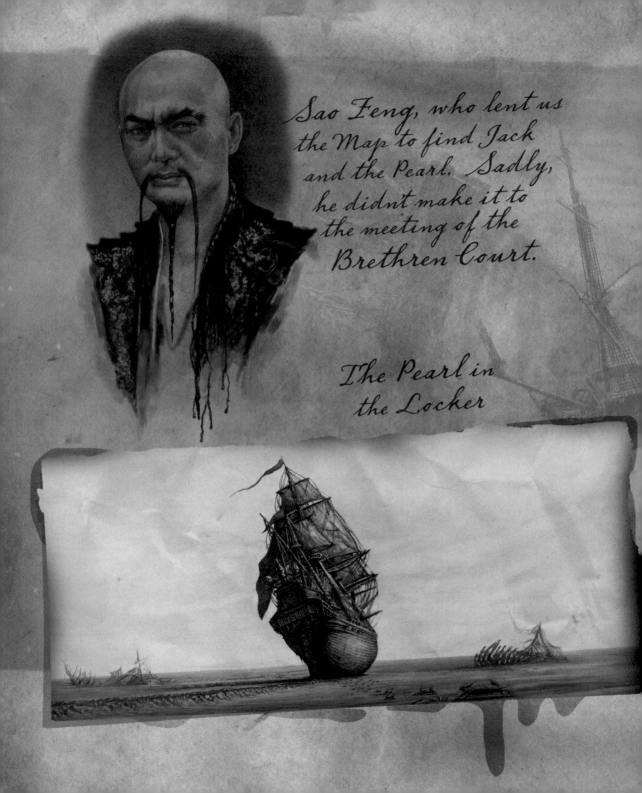

Sao Feng, who lent us
the Map to find Jack
and the Pearl. Sadly,
he didn't make it to
the meeting of the
Brethren Court.

The Pearl in
the Locker

THE FARTHEST GATE

The Farthest Gate will take you to the Land Beyond Death, which includes all incarnations of the afterlife. The location of the gate changes depending on the season and the alignment of the stars. Once you pass through the gate, you will find yourself on a strait of water that will fork into pathways to different spiritual realms.

To rescue Jack Sparrow, we traveled to the Farthest Gate, with a chart that Will Turner borrowed from Sao Feng to lead us to the Edge of the World. There, the seas spilled over into an endlessly long waterfall. Turner wanted to turn back, but Barbossa insisted that the only way to get there was to let the *Hai Peng*, our borrowed ship, run straight and true. I'll never forget the unmistakable roar of the raging waters and the sight of the ocean itself flowing over and down into nothingness.

We landed right at the shore of Davy Jones's Locker. The *Hai Peng* shattered into a million pieces, but we managed to go on and locate Jack. Our trip back aboard the *Pearl* took us over the Locker's dark waters, past a sea teeming with lost souls who Tia Dalma told us should have been in the care of Davy Jones to be ferried to the other side.

The navigational chart that Will Turner borrowed leads to places known and unknown, to the afterlife, and to unexplored worlds. It's made up of a series of rings that can line up many many different ways, which can steer you to places that could have monsters or magic.

I have heard a few stories about how this chart came to be. It seems an ancient Chinese emperor sent out a special cadre of his best explorers to travel to the ends of the earth, seeking the secret knowledge that lies at the far reaches of the world. Their task was to find not just the geographical information, but also to map out the metaphysical and metaphorical realms that could be reached by means other than conventional travel. The explorers, who traveled over endless miles of sea and land, returned years later after countless adventures, to compile the final map and present it to the emperor. The emperor realized the value of the map and instead of making it available to everyone, hid it away to protect its secrets.

I was also told, in an interesting variation on this story, that the explorers came back one hundred years later, not having aged a day.

There was Chinese writing all over it, which Tai Huang (of the Hai Peng) told me were names of possible destinations: the Sea of Stolen Memories, the Thousand Tree Mountains, Blue Dream River, Dancing Sand Beach, and Beautiful Goddess Island—I've got to get the coordinates for that! I also saw pictures on the chart of a tiger, a dragon, and strangely, a little black mouse.

THE GREEN FLASH

The Green Flash signals the return of a soul from the world of the dead. It happens at the last glimpse of sunset—shooting into the sky. Some go their whole lives and never see it. Some claim to have seen it, but have not.

I learned firsthand about the Green Flash when the *Pearl* and her crew (and her captains) were trying to get back from Davy Jones's Locker. We found the right passage—if I can call it that—on the Map to the Land Beyond Death, where it was written: "Over the edge, back over again, sunrise sets at the flash of green." Well, I thought that sunrises don't set. Of course, a sunset is relative to whether you are above or below the ocean—and when we realized what this all meant we were as below as anyone could possibly get.

Jack Sparrow—clever as always—was able to figure what to do. He was playing with the map, turning the rings around, when several Chinese characters lined up and suddenly he could read the words "Up is Down." After that, he started running from port to starboard and back again. Admittedly, his actions could have seemed fairly normal for him and unrelated to our dilemma, but it wasn't long before we discerned his true purpose and joined him, racing from rail to rail, timing it with the water's swells. Cotton let the wheel shift and the ship tilted over. I held my breath as we rotated—almost lost my grip and was floating away when Marty grabbed me. But blessed sweet Westerlies, the ship righted and we gazed upon the most beautiful sunrise I'd ever seen. We had made it back to the land of the living.

TIA DALMA

Tia Dalma was a hoodoo priestess with fathomless powers. This mystic could be found in a small wooden house above the swamps of the Cypress Forest along the Pantano River. There, inside the thick, smothering jungle, bloodwood trees line the banks, their roots spreading like gaping jaws. In and amongst this dire swampland, her devotees could be found, making offerings and burning candles. But these silent acolytes were to be ignored, for they were most certainly in as grievous straits as any seeker who plied the bayou waters.

It was said that Tia Dalma had been practicing her ways since the waters were tamed, but as it is impolite to ask a woman's age, no one was able to confirm that. Let it just be stated that several generations fell under her spell and there are many who could tell interesting tales of their relationships with this enchantress.

She appeared to be an eccentric, but her skills in the realm of magic were exceptional. She could scry (although it was thought inexplicable that she used crab claws for this purpose) and could see through the cloud in a man's mind to his past and his future. It was rumored that she also possessed the ability to return the dead to life. But it was no rumor—she brought back Captain Barbossa to help us navigate the weird and haunted shores at World's End when we went to rescue Captain Jack Sparrow from Davy Jones's Locker.

Tia Dalma was an extremely seductive creature who cast an enticing but tangled net. Her charms did not always effect good fortune, although her abilities were unquestionable. Her knowledge was vast. I learned not to doubt her when she offered protection and never to cross her—she was a strong ally and could be any even stronger enemy.

In order to receive her services, payment was required. This could have been an object of immeasurable value or, if you were fortunate enough to have acquired one, <u>an object of supernatural nature. She was also known to barter</u>. *Why she would want that*

Tia Dalma helped Captain Jack Sparrow in his search for the *wretched* Dead Man's Chest, using her crab claws to scry the location of the *undead* *Flying Dutchman*, and then joined us on our journey to the Realm *monkey,* of the Dead. Later, as we made our way to the convening of the *I'll never* Brethren Court, we learned that her reason for helping us bring *know.* Jack back was not as unselfish as we might have thought. She was, as it turned out, the goddess Calypso bound in human form, and Jack had the last Piece of Eight needed to release her.

I wonder what Jack traded to get that marvelous compass...

Tia Dalma becoming Calypso before the battle with the East India Trading Company.

CALYPSO, GODDESS OF THE SEA

Of Calypso's beauty and power, all sailors were in awe. Her womanliness was unsurpassed in grace and bearing. She was as changeable and whimsical as the sea itself, and exemplified the deepest charity and brilliance of woman's mercurial nature. Calypso's powers were only eclipsed by the great god of the sea Poseidon himself, and only Zeus, chief amongst all gods, could command her.

As with all beings of great might, she was both a nurturer and a destroyer. Calypso had dominion over all the seas, calming troubled waters but also stirring up adversities that vexed all men, reminding us that her inexplicable behavior was a manifestation of the Wild Ways–that which kept us separate from the domesticated society of men on land.

She was the protector of all sailors. It was she who sent forth the *Dutchman* to rescue souls lost at sea. This was the most noble of her mandates, as even the most scurrilous of sea dogs could be granted the opportunity to seek and find forgiveness for their crimes, allowing them to find safe harbor in Fiddler's Green.

As I said earlier, at the First Meeting of the Brethren Court, the Pirate Lords bound Calypso, the Goddess of the Sea, in human form, sealing her fate with Nine Pieces of Eight so that the rule of the seas would belong to men. But in doing so, the now calmed waters became traversable to all seafarers, and the East India Trading Company was able to gradually assert dominion over the world's waterways, exterminating all pirates who stood in their path. In order to fight against this, the Pirate Lord Barbossa suggested that the goddess be unbound, to take our fate back into our own hands. He also hoped that, as her liberators, she would grant us her favor and bring her powers to bear against the EITC.

Most of the Pirate Lords would have liked us to believe that any attempts to seek out Calypso would prove as futile as sailing with a compass that doesn't point North. But Barbossa knew that none other than the mystic Tia Dalma, who lived on the Pantano River, was the human incarnation of the goddess. When we sought to save Jack Sparrow from Davy Jones's Locker, Barbossa persuaded Tia Dalma to join us on this voyage, although it was not until later that we learned the reason why.

After the Pirate Lords voted to go to war against the EITC, Barbossa was able to enact his scheme and release Calypso—fulfilling the deal that he had made with her after she brought him back from the Realm of the Dead. The Pieces of Eight, which we borrowed from the Fourth Meeting, needed to be burned together, on water. Then one needed only to say the incantation, "Calypso, I release you from your human bonds." 'Twas said it must be spoken softly, as if to a lover. Barbossa did all this on the *Pearl* as we sailed to meet Beckett's armada, though Barbossa's declared recitation did not initially work. It was Ragetti who freed the goddess, voicing the words with a genuine love of the sea.

When Tia Dalma was transformed back into Calypso, she grew to ten times her normal size and crashed to the deck of the Pearl as thousands of little crabs. From now on, the only time I want to see those buggers is swimming in a bowl of butter!

THE TREASURE OF ISLA DE MUERTA

On the *Isla de Muerta*—an island that could not be found except by those who already knew where it was—lay a chest filled with 882 pieces of Aztec gold. The gold was blood money, paid to the Spanish conqueror Cortés to stem the slaughter he wreaked upon the indigenous tribes of the New World with his army. But the greed of Cortés was so great that he dishonored the payment and continued his bloodshed to gain even more riches. A legend grew that these actions so angered the heathen gods that they placed a most terrible curse upon the gold.

The legend was confirmed when Captain Jack Sparrow used his compass to locate the island, although he did not actually see the treasure until many years later. His First Mate Barbossa persuaded him to share the coordinates with the crew and then led a mutiny that left Jack marooned on a small tropical spit of land with only a pistol holding a single shot and the knowledge that the treacherous Barbossa and his crew were sailing away with the *Pearl* towards a treasure that would seemingly allow them a free and unfettered life.

Barbossa and his crew frittered the coins away on food and drink and pleasurable company. But the more they gave them away, the more they discovered that drink would not satisfy, food turned to ash in their mouths, and that pleasurable company left them wanting.

The final aspect of the curse, that would reveal their true nature to an unsuspecting eye, was that when moonlight fell across their bodies, they became skeletons. The crew continued plying the waters, learning that, in order to end the curse, all the scattered pieces of gold needed to be restored to the chest and the <u>blood repaid</u>. *The proper blood*

In time, they found all but one piece—the piece that a remorseful crew member, Bootstrap Bill Turner, sent to his son Will. Will set sail to find his father, not knowing that Bootstrap had been sent to the bottom of the sea by the crew for his action. Will's ship was attacked by the *Pearl*, but the boy was rescued by a ship carrying Governor Weatherby Swann and his young daughter Elizabeth, who took the coin fearing that Will would be mistaken for a pirate. It lay hidden in her dresser for ten years before she was compelled to wear it one fateful day in Port Royal—the same day that Captain Jack Sparrow arrived, looking for a fast ship to commandeer.

Elizabeth was captured when the *Pearl* arrived in the port, summoned by the call of the coin. Will Turner, a blacksmith now, threw in with Sparrow to find her (for Will was in love with the lass), and this pursuit eventually ended at *Isla de Muerta*, where the blood debt was paid and the curse was lifted. *Apart from one blasted monkey.*

Isla de Muerta went all pear-shaped after this, and was reclaimed by the sea.

THE BLACK PEARL

You may have heard rumors of a ship with black sails that was so fast it was nigh uncatchable. Many years ago it was said to be crewed by the damned and captained by a man so evil that Hell itself spat him back out. That man was Hector Barbossa, under the curse of the Aztec gold. Sightings of the *Black Pearl* have been reported all over the world, ranging from Madagascar to Newport to Singapore.

One story I've heard whispered is that the *Pearl* was originally the well-known merchant ship the *Wicked Wench*, captained by Jack Sparrow back when he was an honest seaman, ferrying cargo to and from Africa. Cutler Beckett, on behalf of The East India Trading Company, commissioned Captain Sparrow to pick up a cargo, which Jack agreed to do. But when he found out that the cargo was human, Jack refused to be involved. Furious with Jack's unwillingness to close the deal, Beckett tracked down the ship and set her ablaze. She sank to a watery grave.

Not much is known about the events that occurred after that, as much of Jack's past is mired in a thick fog. Somewhere in the midst of all of it, Beckett unjustly branded Jack a pirate, leaving a mark that had nothing to do with Jack's past, but would have everything to do with his future.

Jack loves that ship more than his own life. That's why he made a bargain with Davy Jones—and I wish I'd been there to witness the negotiations!—to raise the ship from the bottom of the ocean, but neither he nor the ship were the same since. She emerged a ghost ship, her sails tattered and her hull blackened. Jack renamed her the *Black Pearl* and turned to a life of piracy. In return for Jack's soul, Jones allowed him to captain the *Pearl* for thirteen years. Sadly for Jack, the ship was taken from him after only two years when his First Mate Barbossa led a mutiny.

After many years, Jack got his ship back, but went down with her when the Kraken pulled her down to Davy Jones's Locker. He came back up with it—and Barbossa—when he was rescued. It's been a constant battle between the two "Captains" ever since.

Jack may have fallen behind but I could not follow the Code and leave him behind.

Only the Flying
Dutchman is
faster than the
Pearl when the
wind is
against her.

DAVY JONES AND THE FLYING DUTCHMAN

For many years, there was a legend that, when a sailor was faced with a watery grave due to shipwreck, illness, desperation, or other calumnity, Davy Jones would appear and offer him the chance to delay his Final Judgment by serving on the *Flying Dutchman*, an immortal ship that can travel above or below the waves. Contractual terms were typically one soul, bound to crew a lifetime on the *Dutchman*. Other contracts extended to one hundred years or an eternity.

While this option allowed the sailor to avoid death, his fate would actually prove to be much worse, as an eternity of servitude on that loathsome ship was just as close to losing one's soul as is being delivered not to Heaven but to that fiery place of infernal unhappiness. And as time passed, the crew member would become more of the sea than of man—barnacled, transformed, and eventually part of the *Flying Dutchman* itself.

Here is the history of Davy Jones so far as I have been able to surmise it: Jones was once a man, like any other man. It was said that he was charged by the goddess Calypso to look after those who had died at sea and to ferry them to the other side—a noble deed. Every ten years, he would be granted the opportunity to come ashore and be with Calypso, whom he loved.

But at the end of the ten years, when he went to meet her, she did not appear. His love betrayed, he corrupted his purpose, and his own body became corrupted as well.

It was Jones who told the Brethren Court how to bind Calypso into human form. He never stopped loving her and the pain it caused him was too much to live with but not enough to cause him to die. In his madness and grief, he carved out his own heart, locked it up in a chest, and hid the chest from the world, buried on *Isla Cruces*. He kept the key to that chest close to where his heart once was.

Jones also had a Kraken at his disposal that would find and take you down to his Locker, a place of unimaginable torment.

Occasionally, when a deal was being struck with Jones, an accord could be reached that would temporarily defer the time to be served and grant the seeker's urgent desire, such as the raising and captaincy of a sunken ship or the retrieval and marriage to a lost loved one, but such actions were consequential and payment could not be avoided. It was not a matter of how long until he came after you, it was a matter of how long before you were found.

Rarely could the afflicted's fate be avoided. However, there were cases when a new deal was struck upon the first deal's termination, to substitute the soul of the selected individual with an agreed-upon amount of alternate souls. The worth of the individual's soul was determined by Jones himself.

The *Dutchman* sails as its Captain commands. But the crew is not bound to the Captain; they are bound to the *Dutchman*. Whoever controls the heart of the Captain of the *Dutchman* controls the Seven Seas (and by extension its crew). I learned that whoever holds the heart has the power to free the doomed souls enslaved as crewmen. But Jones took care to keep the heart beating, for whosoever stabs the heart of the *Dutchman*'s Captain will take his place.

I witnessed all the above with my own eyes. After the Brethren Court voted to make war against the fleet assembled by the EITC, Jones—the terrible haunted man—nay—shell of a man—would have wreaked havoc on the innocent and destroyed the pirate fleet without quarter, for he was a soulless brute and controlled by duplicitous bilge rats. We all would have died in the fierce battle had not the heart Jones protected, so fiercely and so undeservedly, been destroyed by the thrust of a sword—a sword that the bearer himself crafted in an earlier life and then used of his own free accord! And so the duty of the Captain of the *Flying Dutchman* was passed to another and all were saved.

Nowadays, when I see the flash of green off the rolling waters, I think of those fortunate souls who are passing to their reward, shepherded by a fair and noble Captain whose heart is truly in the right place. At my final hour, I'll be glad if I am given the chance to shake his hand and tell him what a good man he is. But just the same, he'd better greet me with some rum!

Take What You Can— Give Nothing Back!

THE BOOK'S PRODUCERS WOULD LIKE TO EXTEND THEIR GRATITUDE TO THE AMAZING ARTISTS WHO CONTRIBUTED HEREIN.

Page 7 — Pirates characters by James Ward Byrkit

Pages 8-9 — Pirate Lords by Mark "Crash" McCreery

Pages 10-11 — Map of the Brethren Court by Bret Healey, David Kim, Rich Tuzon, and Ronald Velasquez

Page 14, left — Visual development of Bootstrap Bill by Crash McCreery

Page 17 — Art by Wayne Lo

Page 20 — Jack Sparrow's gun by Jessica Ward

Page 22-23 — Will Turner and Barbossa's swords and Figure A. by Jessica Ward

Page 24-25 — Battle scene by Simon Murton

Page 27 — Hand by Jessica Ward. Dice by Crash McCreery

Page 29 — Guitar and pennywhistle by Jessica Ward

Page 31 — Costume sketch for Captain Barbossa by Darrell Warner

Page 34 — Jack Sparrow tattoo by Ken Diaz

Page 35 — Ayer's Hair Vigor advertisement from the collection of Jody Revenson

Page 41 — Coconut Tree by Jessica Ward

Page 42 — Fishing Lure by Jessica Ward

Text by Monique Peterson, Jody Revenson, and Jessica Ward
Designed by Jon Glick, mouse+tiger

For information address Disney Editions, 114 Fifth Avenue,
New York, New York 10011-5690.
Editorial Director: Wendy Lefkon
Senior Editor: Jody Revenson
Editorial Assistant: Jessica Ward

Pirates of the Caribbean: The Curse of the Black Pearl
Screen Story by Ted Elliott & Terry Rossio and Stuart Beattie and Jay Wolpert
Screenplay by Ted Elliott & Terry Rossio

Pirates of the Caribbean: Dead Man's Chest
Pirates of the Caribbean: At World's End
Based on characters created by Ted Elliott & Terry Rossio
and Stuart Beattie and Jay Wolpert
Written by Ted Elliott & Terry Rossio

Produced by Jerry Bruckheimer
Directed by Gore Verbinski
Based on Walt Disney's Pirates of the Caribbean

The book's producers would like to thank the following for their contributions to this book: Jennifer Banzaca, Christine Cadena, Guy Cunningham, Sharon Krinsky, Mitchell Leib, Kevin Monroe, Dan Owen, Jon Rogers, Erik Schmudde, and Marybeth Tregarthen.

Library of Congress Cataloging-in-Publication Data on File
ISBN 13: 978-1-4231-0654-8
ISBN 10: 1-4231-0654-7
Printed in the United States
First Edition
10 9 8 7 6 5 4 3 2

DisneyPirates.Com